The Adventure of Money
A Guide to Saving, Budgeting, & Investing

Written by

Annette Harris

Edited by

Dweise Harris

To my readers, this book could not have been realized without your recognition of the critical need for financial literacy within our communities. Thank you for your encouragement.

Table of Contents

Introduction: The World of Money

Welcome to The World of Money! In this journey, we will explore everything about money—why you need it and even why you desire it. First, we will explore the basics: how to earn money, spend it wisely, and save for the future. Then, get ready to be inspired! We will meet some incredible people who have turned their dreams into reality, and you might discover the path to achieving your own.

Saving money can be an exciting adventure! You can put your coins in a piggy bank, open a savings account at the bank, or even invest it to watch it grow! Saving money takes a little patience and discipline, but before you know it, you will have enough cash to buy something awesome without asking for help from anyone else, like your parents or friends.

Get ready for your thrilling financial journey because "The Adventure of Money" is here to be your ultimate guide to discovering the treasure of financial freedom!

Let's dive in and unlock the secrets to making your money work for you!

What is Money?

Money is a method of payment accepted by buyers (you) and sellers for goods and services. In other words, the buyer gives the seller money in exchange for something the buyer wants to purchase, like candy, toys, tickets, gifts, etc. This is a simple trade or exchange.

Have you ever gone to the store and wanted to buy a new toy, a new shirt, or a brand-new pair of shoes? Well, it all costs money. Just like you need a ticket to get into the movie theater or ride a rollercoaster, you need money to buy a toy, shirt, shoes, or even a special ice cream treat. Money helps us buy the things we want or need. With money, you can purchase all sorts of fun and exciting things or use it to pay bills.

What are the different forms of money?

Around the world, money comes in different shapes and sizes. We have shiny coins and colorful paper money that we often call 'bills.'

In the United States, our paper money is green and called bills, and we also have shiny coins. Coins are small, round pieces of metal, and they are usually made of copper, nickel, or silver. The front of coins often has a picture of a famous person or a landmark. For example, the United States dime has a picture of President Franklin D. Roosevelt on one side and a torch, olive branch, and oak branch on the other.

How do you determine the value of a coin? The value of a coin – how much it is worth – is decided by its size, color, and the picture on it.

In the United States, the coin's value is printed right on it. Here are some common coins along with their values: one cent (a penny, worth 1¢), five cents (a nickel, worth 5¢), ten cents (a dime, worth 10¢), twenty-five cents (a quarter, worth 25¢), fifty cents (a half dollar, worth 50¢), and one dollar (a dollar coin or silver/golden dollar, worth $1.00).

I often get asked the question, "Can paper money grow on trees?" The answer is no. Paper money is made from a unique blend of materials and comes in various colors and sizes. In the United States, it is crafted from linen and cotton. This composition enhances its durability and helps prevent **counterfeiting**, a process that happens when someone attempts to create fake money.

Money looks different in every country. Paper money often shows important people, buildings, or natural sights. Did you know that Martha Washington is the only woman to have appeared on paper money in the United States? In 2030, Harriet Tubman will become the second woman to appear on paper money in the United States. However, she will be the first African American woman with this honor. She will be featured on the $20 bill.

How can you determine the value of paper money? Like coins, the denomination is printed in large letters and numbers on the bill. The most common denominations you will encounter are $1, $5, $10, $20, $50, and $100.

What about plastic money?

Sometimes, we use special cards, known as "plastic money," like debit or credit cards, to make purchases. When you use a debit card, you are spending money already in your bank account; it is your income or savings. In contrast, when you use a credit card, you borrow money that is not yours and will need to pay it back. If you do not pay off the entire amount you borrowed at once, you will have to repay interest. **Interest** is the extra money you pay a company for borrowing money. For example, if you used a credit card to buy something for $20, you might have to repay $22 due to interest. That is why using credit cards only when you can afford to pay the money back is so important.

Why we need money: To fulfill our needs and wants

My daughter always used to ask me, "Can't we just go get what we want?" This was before she understood how money was earned. I would respond that I have to work for my money and decide how to spend it on our needs and wants. This was not always easy to explain. So, I found a few reasons why we need money that might make it easier for her to understand.

We need money to purchase things like food, gas for a vehicle, toys, backpacks for school, video games, and more. Many things we buy with money fall into the categories of needs and wants. Needs are things people require to survive. For example, we need to eat and use money to buy food that nourishes our bodies. We also need a place to live (shelter), and money pays for that. These are all considered 'needs.' On the other hand, you might want a new bike or a video game. These items are not necessary to live. So, they are called 'wants.' A want is something nice to have, but it is not required.

Needs vs. Wants: Sorting Out Your Wishes

We all have some important needs. These essential needs include food, shelter, and clothing. It is important to understand that not all food, types of shelter, and clothing are necessary, but they may sometimes be desired. You might want ice cream or a chocolate bar, but these are not essential foods. However, they would taste really good, especially an ice cream with a cherry on top. You may also want a large house with a balcony and a pool in the backyard, but large houses can be expensive and require significant savings. Do not forget that brand name clothing can be very pricey compared to what you can find at a local shop. It all sounds and looks nice, but separating your needs from your wants is important when deciding what you can afford.

Needs: Food, Shelter, Clothing

As a child, your parents may buy groceries or food from a restaurant to provide you with nourishing meals for your body. Eating out at restaurants is convenient but expensive. Buying groceries from the store is important so that meals last long. It also reduces what your parents pay for food. If you want to learn more about meal planning, ask an adult how you can help plan the weekly meals. This can help them save money and time and ensure that you have healthier options for fueling your body.

Shelter means the place that you live in. This can vary for a lot of people. You could live in an apartment, a condo, a home, or a duplex with family members. Shelter is an expensive need, and the bigger your home is, the more it costs to maintain it. Your parents have to pay rent or mortgage every month so you can have a place to stay, including utilities, like the water bill, the electric bill, or even cable.

Finally, clothing is an important need to help ensure you have the necessities to keep you warm and comfortable. Different brands can cost different amounts of money. Basic clothing, such as shirts, pants, underwear, socks, and shoes, can be very affordable. However, focusing on specific clothing brands can cost your parents lots of money.

When I was younger, I saved my allowance to afford name brand clothes. There was also one pair of shoes that I really wanted, but my mom would not buy them for me. However, she provided me with a monthly allowance of $20, and I saved some of my money to have enough to purchase the shoes. I also used some of my money to purchase after-school snacks. My goal was to have the new shoes by the time the new school year came around. For months, I saved my money and was finally able to buy the shoes. It was very rewarding to save and purchase brand name clothing on my own and walk into school wearing something I earned myself.

Wants

Your basic needs for food, shelter, and clothing are essential, but what about the things we desire, like toys, games, or trips to amusement parks?

There are enjoyable things we wish to have, which are categorized as wants. Wants are items we do not necessarily need but would make life more enjoyable. For instance, have you ever been to a store while your parents were grocery shopping and seen a new game or toy that caught your eye? Did you ask for that game or toy and wonder why you did not receive it? It may not have been in your parents' budget. You might have questioned why they could not purchase it right then and felt disappointed. However, since this game or toy was not a need, your parents may not have had the funds allocated in their budget for that purchase. Or perhaps they were saving up for your birthday or holiday gifts.

Prioritizing Needs Over Wants

When your parents did not buy that new game, it might not have been the answer you were looking for, but they were ensuring that your needs were met while shopping for groceries for the family or saving money to cover the monthly bills. Sometimes, adults must make tough decisions to ensure your basic needs are met. Your wants can be fulfilled when there is money available in your parents' budget, but they are not guaranteed.

Chapter 1: Earning Your Own Money

Allowance

Now that we have covered the basics of money, how can you earn it? Your parents may give you an allowance, or you could earn it on your own. An allowance is money given either on a regular basis or for a specific task to help someone pay or save for their needs and wants.

Earning an allowance and how much allowance you earn can vary. Your allowance could be $1.00 a week, $5.00 a week, $10.00 a month, or more. You may receive your allowance without doing anything at all, which is a gift that you can use for your future goals. Or, you may have to do chores around the house to receive an allowance.

My neighbor's children, Stephanie and John, each earned a $5.00 weekly allowance by completing a variety of chores. Stephanie was responsible for feeding the family's two dogs, Buster and Bella, cleaning the litter boxes of the family's two cats, Mittens and Patches, and vacuuming the entire house. John's responsibilities included taking out the trash and recycling every week, as well as helping his dad wash the car on Saturdays. Their parents believed these tasks were important contributions to the household, so they considered a $5.00 allowance to be fair. Stephanie and John enjoyed doing their chores because they loved their pets and being outdoors. They also appreciated receiving the allowance they earned after completing their chores.

Earning an allowance offers so many more benefits than just receiving money. Earning an allowance for the chores and tasks that you have completed is very fulfilling. When assigned certain chores and tasks, you learn the importance of correctly completing the job and earning your reward. This helps you grow by developing a sense of responsibility. It also helps foster independence, self-esteem, and a sense of accomplishment while contributing to developing a strong work ethic. Earning an allowance also helps you learn financial responsibility. It helps you understand and appreciate the value of money and how to manage your money (saving and budgeting). No matter how you earn your allowance, it is important to set goals and save it in a piggy bank or a savings account for your future wants and needs.

Chore Challenges

You can earn an allowance by doing chores around the house. Some chores, such as cleaning your room, washing your clothes, bathing the dog, or sweeping the floor, may be standard tasks for which your parents do not give you an allowance. However, if you think creatively, you might discover additional chores for which you can earn an allowance and suggest them to your parents.

Washing a car can be tricky, especially if it is really dirty. If you wash the car every month, you might earn an allowance! Talk to your parents about taking on this chore. This includes washing, drying, and even vacuuming the inside to clean out the dirt. If they agree to give you an allowance, find out how many times you need to wash the car each month to earn it.

Cutting the grass is another difficult job. If you learn how to use lawn equipment safely, you might be able to do this job by yourself. Many people do it alone or hire someone else to do it. If you take over this job, you could help your parents save time and money. Over time, you will learn useful techniques and gain valuable skills. Once you get good at it, you could even earn extra money by cutting lawns in your neighborhood. This could become your **side hustle**.

Side Hustle Heroes

Starting your own small business while completing your regular chores or work is called a side hustle. A side hustle can help you bring in additional **income** to help you afford your needs and wants. There are many types of side hustles you can think about to help you create your own business.

It's important to think about what skills you may have or how you can use your knowledge to help others. Some skills that people use are crocheting, yard work, tutoring, and more.

Here are some additional ways to earn extra money:

- Babysitting
- Dog Walking

- Pet Sitting
- Owning a Lemonade Stand
- Baking and Selling Cookies

Stephanie started a dog grooming business to help her pay for presents for her family. Stephanie asked her parents if she could go to the neighbor's houses to see if they would pay her to bathe their pets. When they agreed, Stephanie and her parents went door-to-door to ask neighbors if they would be interested in her bathing their dogs for a price. Some neighbors said no, but others agreed and paid Stephanie to bathe their dogs every two weeks. With all the money Stephanie earned, she saved it for the presents she wanted to buy for her parents' birthdays.

Read more about Stephanie's journey in Chapter 5.

John helped his mom plant vegetables and maintained the yard by cutting the grass. As he learned about all the techniques, like cutting grass, edging the sidewalk, and weed-eating the yard, he felt confident enough to begin helping his neighbors for a price. Many of John's neighbors already had their lawn equipment and gas for the machines, so all he had to do was show up, start the machines, and mow the grass. John enjoyed the money he earned through his hard work, which allowed him to buy a new video game he had been eying.

Read more about John's journey in Chapter 6.

The Power of Hard Work

You can find out how amazing things can be when you try hard. Like Stephanie and John, you can reach your savings goals by working hard, being creative, and not giving up.

Remember that wishing for the newest car or the coolest pair of shoes will not magically bring them to you. You will need to take steps to make your dreams come true. Whether helping with chores at home or using your talents to start your own small business, you can achieve your money goals.

So, get ready to work hard, use your skills, and feel the incredible satisfaction of reaching your goals through effort and determination.

Chapter 2: Spending Smart – Making Your Money Count

Okay, picture this: You're itching for that *one thing.* Maybe it's a cool new video game, a pair of sneakers you saw in the store window, a crazy hoodie sweatshirt that screams "you," or an awesome art set for drawing your favorite characters. You can see it in your hands.

Then, you check your pockets, piggy bank, and even under your bed, only to find that you have spent all your allowance, birthday money, and everything else! Poof! Every last cent has vanished. Where did it all go? It's like a mystery; you are the detective trying to figure out where you spent your money.

We all do it at some time, and Jessica and Jasmine knew that feeling too well. They spent their money on a new movie, which was fun and all, but now...the book fair was coming, packed with amazing books they desperately wanted, and their pockets were as empty as a ghost town.

Learning to spend money wisely is an important life skill. This chapter will review how you can become a savvy spender. We will explore the power of budgeting, which is like creating a plan for how you will spend your money. You will learn to track your spending to see what you spend your money on and discover ways to resist buying things you may regret later.

Just imagine – you could have enough money to buy the video game you have been dreaming of, save for a new pair of skates or that cool new trick bike you have seen on television. By learning to spend your money wisely, you can make your money work for you. Whether saving for a future purchase or just enjoying your hard-earned cash responsibly, you will learn how to make choices that align with your goals.

Let's learn how to spend wisely and make your money count.

Budgeting Basics: Your Money Map

Here is how to create a simple budget to plan your spending.

1. **Figure out how much money you have coming in.**

   a. **What money do you have coming in?** Is it from your allowance, money earned from chores, cash gifts from your birthday, or money you have earned from your new small business? You will need to determine how often you receive your money. Is it weekly or monthly, or a combination of both? For example, you could receive a weekly or monthly allowance of $5.00 and receive money from your business every week.

b. **Write everything down.** Details are very important. Use a journal or a computer to keep track of all your money sources and how much you get from each one. For example, you might earn $25 for mowing one neighbor's lawn and $30 for another. This is simple record-keeping.

Write down who gave you the money, the date you got it, and how much it was. This will help you keep track of all the cash coming in. Even if you get money during the holidays, write that down, too. Everything counts!

2. **Track the money you spend.**

   a. **Where does your money go?** Every time you spend money, write down where you spend it. Also, write down what you purchased. You could have bought a new book at the book fair, gotten a haircut, or purchased snacks at the grocery store. Write everything down and subtract what you spent from your income. This might seem like a lot of work, but it helps to know where your money goes and how much you have left. Remember, basic record-keeping and details are both very important.

3. **Create Your Budget!** Now that you have tracked your income and spending, it is time to create your budget so you can plan your spending. You have probably realized that a few of your purchases should not have been made, which is okay. It is about learning from your spending habits and identifying the needs and wants we discussed in the Introduction to the World of Money. To create your budget, identify your needs and wants.

a. **Needs:** As a reminder, needs are the items you absolutely need, like food for mealtime, transportation (a bike to get you back and forth to school), and maybe some school supplies – the basics of life. Needs are typically where you spend most of your money.

b. **Wants:** These are things you would like to have, such as ice cream, toys, or tickets to the carnival. They would be nice to have and make life more fun, but they are not required.

4. **Divide your money!** Dividing your money shows how much you will spend on your needs, wants, and savings. Imagine you receive $20 a week for your allowance. How will you break it down?

Here is an example for dividing your $20 allowance:

a. **Needs ($10):** This is half of your $20 and can be used for things you need, like school lunches or paper.

b. **Wants ($6):** This is for the fun things you like to do or for yummy snacks.

c. **Savings ($4):** This is the leftover money you can save for emergencies or future dreams.

Category	Amount
Needs	$10
Wants	$6
Savings	$4
Total	**$20**

Why does saving money matter? It is always important to set aside some money for savings and not spend it all as soon as you receive it. Imagine seeing a cool toy you want. If you have been saving, you will have the money to buy it! Or maybe your bike gets a flat tire. If you have savings, you can fix it without any stress. Your savings are your contingency funds: money for unexpected problems that may arise.

5. **Plan how you will spend it.** Planning how to spend your money is important because it helps you understand what you are saving for. Whether it is new school clothes, a trip to the amusement park, or sports equipment for the next school year, having a financial goal keeps you focused and motivated while reminding you of the reason behind your savings. Additionally, sticking to your spending and savings plan is crucial to avoid overspending your money. While it can be okay to go over budget sometimes, it should not happen regularly.

6. **Make adjustments.** If your budget is not working, it is time to review it and make changes.

   a. Take some time each week or month to review your spending habits. Reflect on whether you stayed within your budget or overspent. Consider if that shopping trip was a budget buster and ask yourself if it was just a one-time purchase or if it might happen more frequently.

b. If you need to make adjustments because you overspent on clothing, try making adjustments in another area. For example, if you bought a new shirt and also planned to go to a restaurant, think about not going to the restaurant so you can stick to your budget. On the other hand, if you save more than you expected, you can reward yourself with something special, or you can increase how much money you save.

Ultimately, budgeting is not about avoiding spending your money; it is about making wise choices so you can enjoy what you desire while also saving for your future goals.

Impulse Buying: The Sneaky Shopper

Impulse buying is like a sneaky magician who does tricks; you do not know how it happened. The same thing can happen with your money. You can spend it, and it just disappears, and you do not even realize it until it is gone (especially if you are not keeping records of your spending habits).

Remember Jessica and Jasmine and their empty pockets? Jessica and Jasmine had been looking forward to the book fair since they marked it on their calendars at the start of the school year. They had spent the year saving just enough money to buy the amazing books they desperately wanted.

However, over the weekend, Jessica and Jasmine walked by the movie theater and saw the colorful poster for the new movie. It had all their favorite actors. It was action-packed with plenty of epic explosions. It looked very exciting. Their brains went into "Ooh, shiny!" mode. Suddenly, they were reaching for their money, and before they knew it, they were sitting in the movie theater eating popcorn.

Jessica and Jasmine were tricked by impulse buying. They did not stop to think about the book fair and how much they wanted those books; instead, they were distracted by the cool new movie they saw. Ultimately, they regretted passing up the book fair, as they realized it was challenging to control their spending.

Here are some tips to help you avoid similar situations and keep your spending on track with your goals.

Resisting the Urge to Spend Your Money

The *30-second rule* is a helpful strategy for those tempted to make impulsive purchases. Here is how it works: If you find yourself wanting to buy something unplanned while in a store, pause for 30 seconds to consider your decision. During this time, ask yourself: "Do I really need this?" "Is it in my budget?" "What will I do with it?" Although it may seem short, this 30-second pause can give you time to resist the urge to shop impulsively.

Shopping online can also lead to unexpected spending. To avoid this, consider using the *"sleep on it" rule*. When you find clothing, games, or other items you like, leave them in your cart for a day or two before finalizing your purchase. When you return, you may realize that the impulse purchase is not appealing anymore. If that is the case, you can remove it and save your money for something else. However, if you still want the item, proceed with the checkout and look forward to your new purchase.

Finally, you can *"ask a friend first."* Ask someone else what they think about the purchase. You may find that they believe it is too expensive, that you do not need it, or suggest something else instead. If they know your savings goals, they can also remind you of what you are saving for to ensure you stay on track and motivated.

The Importance of Waiting Before Buying

Okay, let's talk about **delayed gratification**. Imagine walking past a store with tons of cheap, flimsy toys. You see a little plastic robot that looks okay. You could buy it right now and have a lot of fun! But what if you did not?

What if you thought about the giant LEGO spaceship you have been dreaming about instead? The one with all the cool pieces and flashing lights?

What if you resisted purchasing something awesome that you see right now, like the little robot, and saved up for the LEGO spaceship? That is called delayed gratification. It means waiting for something bigger and better.

Think of saving your money like saving your boosters in a video game. You can use your one booster now or wait until you have more and zoom past the other cars, helping you cross the finish line faster.

So, what does delayed gratification, the 30-second rule, sleeping on it, and "asking a friend" do for you? These concepts help you build self-control, achieve your future goals, and teach you patience.

You can improve your self-control by finding ways to make better decisions that will help you in the future. Focusing on school and reaching your goals will be easier with better self-control. Plus, as you start making smarter choices, you can become more patient with yourself and others.

Saving money for larger purchases can help you reach your long-term goals, whether saving for next year's fair, buying a new skateboard, or even saving for college or a car! With your newfound patience, you will enjoy the feeling of working hard and achieving your goals.

By avoiding impulse purchases and waiting for what you want, you can be a smart spender and understand that your dreams and goals are possible.

Chapter 3: Saving for the Future – Growing Your Money

If you could have or do anything you wanted in five years, with no limit, what would it be? Maybe it is owning a new bike, having a drum set that helps you create music, or even visiting the NASA space center to experience a shuttle launch.

Take a moment to imagine living your dream! What are you doing? How does it make you feel? Are you hanging out with friends, or are you doing this alone? Are you smiling? Just how exciting is your dream? Think about the steps you took to make it real. Maybe you saved up your money and planned everything out.

However, you achieved it! You are the star of your journey and that dream. It is proof of what you can achieve when you have a plan, practice patience, and believe that you can accomplish your goal.

The Power of Saving

Saving money can be very powerful. When you save, you can see your money grow over time. Sticking to your saving goals helps you make good money choices that match what you want in life. Plus, saving enables you to become better at managing your money.

James and Joe wanted to visit a museum with treasures from around the world. They pictured themselves holding the artifacts and being transported to another time. They knew they had to save money to go on this incredible adventure together. As they saved for their goal, they both maintained a positive attitude about saving their money and made sure that they both stayed on track when there was something new they wanted to purchase. They maintained their self-control and used the *"ask a friend first"* rule to stay on track.

By maintaining a positive attitude, James and Joe devised a plan to save for what they both desired. This approach enabled them to make financial decisions that aligned with their goals. Although saving money was uncharted territory, they were confident they could embark on this journey with each other's support and realize their biggest dreams!

Setting Savings Goals

Be "SMART"

When it comes to saving, setting clear goals is important. Writing your goals down is like having a map that shows where you want to go! For your goals to be effective, they should be unique to what you want, need, and value. They should also be "SMART":

Specific: Clearly define what you want to accomplish.
Measurable: Keep track of your progress (weekly, monthly, yearly)
Achievable: Ensure your goal is possible.
Realistic: Set a goal that you can reach.
Time-Bound: Give yourself a deadline.

Making SMART goals helps you see how you are doing, stay excited, ensure your goals are possible, and set deadlines to keep you focused.

Fuel for Motivation

Setting savings goals can help you dream big. A goal gives you something to work towards, making all your efforts worthwhile. Think about the last race you ran: What motivated you to push forward to the finish line? Was it to finish before someone else? Did you want to earn a medal? Or did you want to finish the race with pride? Just like finishing a race is satisfying, setting a savings goal helps you see why and what you are saving for.

Direction and Focus

Goals provide direction and focus, whether they are big or small. They allow you to create a roadmap that helps you track your achievements and plan for the future. For example, if you want to save $600 for a new TV in six months, saving $100 each month will get you to your goal.

Setting a deadline helps you focus your energy and money toward a specific goal, so you do not drift aimlessly. If your goal is to save money each month and you miss a deadline, the goal will help you determine whether you are on track or off track and clarify what you are working toward.

Building Confidence

When was the last time you achieved a goal? Think about how you felt at that moment. Did you earn an 'A' on an assignment? Did you win a race? Did you land that job you really wanted? Reflect on your feelings after you achieved it. Did you feel accomplished? Did you feel as if you could conquer anything that came your way?

Reaching savings goals can make you feel accomplished and boost your self-confidence. Even small savings goals can inspire you to set and reach bigger goals in other areas of your life. Every time you take a step toward a bigger dream; it strengthens your belief in what you can achieve in the future.

Resiliency in the Face of Challenges

Have you ever heard the saying, "Minor setbacks can lead to major comebacks?" When you set a goal, you may encounter obstacles that slow down your progress. However, having a strong reason – a "why" (like saving for a car) – can motivate you to continue through obstacles. It is important to remember that you might stumble and fall victim to impulsive shopping, but learning from your mistakes will help you become strong when facing challenges. When you recover from your financial mistakes, obstacles can become temporary hurdles rather than impossible walls to climb.

Dreaming Big – Potential and Opportunities

Dreaming big helps you learn how to save now and prepares you for success later in life. The reward is much more satisfying when you practice delayed gratification and wait a little longer to get what you truly want! Imagine how good it will feel to purchase something new with your money, knowing you put in the time and effort to achieve your goal.

By dreaming big, you can identify future opportunities that will make you an expert at budgeting, capable of making smart choices, and someone who understands that true happiness comes from achieving your goals rather than keeping up with others.

Your Savings, Your Freedom, Your Future

Saving money gives you the freedom to choose how and what to spend it on. It can also help you become financially independent to take control of your life and manage future purchases. Imagine not having to rely on others to pay for things you can afford to buy.

For example, if you want to buy a video game, a new pair of shoes, a car, or a book, every dollar you save helps you reach your goal. Think of each dollar as a brick in the foundation of your future. The bigger your savings goal, the stronger your foundation will be, making it more important to start saving now.

Reward Yourself by Celebrating Your Wins

As you reach your goals, it is very important to celebrate the milestones you have achieved. Rewarding yourself does not have to be extravagant or expensive. You can treat yourself to something simple, like enjoying an ice cream cone, watching a new movie, reading a book, or spending time at the park. These enjoyable activities can keep you motivated and focused on your goals. Treating yourself makes saving fun and may help you achieve your goals faster.

Be an Inspiration to Others

When you set and save for your goals, you can inspire others. Your hard work, passion, and planning prove that anything is possible. You can help others learn how to save by sharing your experiences. You can also support them as they work towards their goals. Remind them of what they are saving for and talk about possible challenges and opportunities that may arise.

Saving Strategies

There are many ways to save money. You can keep extra money in a piggy bank, put it in a savings account, or follow the **50/30/20 Budget Rule** to manage your spending and savings. While these three methods are among the most common, there are lots of other options, too. Let's look at different ways to help find what works best for you.

Piggy Bank Power

Using a piggy bank is a classic way to save money. A great example is James and Joe, who saved for their NASA space adventure. They both needed to save $120 to buy a ticket and an astronaut action figure as a memento of their fun adventure at the space station. They wanted to watch their savings grow, so they used clear piggy banks to track their progress toward their goal.

James and Joe aimed to have enough money saved by May, the end of the school year, to have an amazing summer adventure. On their birthdays, which were just a few months apart, they decided to put half of the money they received from their parents and relatives right into their piggy banks. They also saved $3.00 out of their weekly allowance of $5.00, showing their determination to stick to their goal.

Starting in August, James and Joe were excited to see what they had saved by January. They were thrilled to discover that their hard work had paid off. Thanks to the clever savings strategy and discipline, they each saved over $60. In fact, when they counted the money saved in their piggy banks, they found they each had more than $80!

Throughout the school year, James and Joe shared their savings progress and celebrated by playing video games, which excited them even more as they inched closer and closer to their goal. Thanks to their saving habits, they each saved more than $140 in their piggy banks by the end of May. With big smiles and hearts full of anticipation, they felt proud and ready for the adventure they had worked so hard for.

James and Joe's parents and siblings were thrilled to see their dedication to saving. To celebrate their commitment and inspire them further, they surprised them with a bright pair of astronaut socks covered with images of colorful planets and stars, showing them that saving can lead to limitless possibilities.

Overwhelmed with excitement, James and Joe wanted to learn more about managing their money. They approached their parents with curiosity, asking if they could open a savings account to keep their hard-earned money safe and how it could grow **compound interest**. Their parents happily agreed, seeing it as an excellent chance for the boys to learn about the magic of savings accounts!

Savings Account Magic

Besides using piggy banks, another smart way to keep your money safe is to deposit it into a savings account. Let's compare piggy banks to savings accounts.

You can put money into piggy banks for safekeeping and to save for something special. You can do the same thing with a savings account.

However, with a savings account, when you deposit money into them, you can earn *'extra money'* on the money you deposit into them. You do not earn 'extra money' when you put your money in a piggy bank. This *'extra money'* is known as compound interest.

So, savings accounts are a smart way to keep your money safe while allowing it to grow. Like a piggy bank, you can deposit money into a savings account as you save for something special. But, unlike a piggy bank, when you put your money in a savings account, you can earn interest on it, which is called compound interest.

Compound interest helps you earn even more money while you save. How does it work? When you deposit money into a savings account, the bank pays you for allowing them to hold your money. It is the bank's way of saying "thank you" for trusting us with your savings.

For example, if you put $100 into a savings account with a 2% monthly interest rate, at the end of the first month, you would earn $2 in interest. This brings your new account balance to $102. When the next month starts, and you still have $102 in your account, the bank will again pay you 2% interest on that amount. This means you would earn $2.04 in interest for the second month, and your new balance would be $104.04. Isn't that amazing?

All you had to do was let the bank hold your money in a savings account.

Here is how you can understand the power of compounding interest when you save $100 at different interest rates.

Interest	Month 1	Month 2	Month 3
2%	$102.00	$104.04	$106.12
3%	$103.00	$106.09	$109.27
4%	$104.00	$108.16	$112.49

Every month, the money in your savings account, along with the money you continue to add, earns more interest, which continues to compound and grow. That means the longer you save, the more money you will have for your goals.

To save your money, you can save it in two of the most common types of accounts: traditional savings accounts and high-yield savings accounts. So, what type of savings account can you choose from?

Traditional Savings Accounts

Regular savings accounts are the most common type of bank account. They let you easily take out your money when you want it and safely earn compound interest. One of the best things about a regular savings account is that you do not need a lot of money to start one. Some banks let you open one with just $25! This way, you can start saving and watching your money grow!

High-Yield Savings Accounts

Another option for saving money is a high-yield savings account. Most banks allow you to open one if you have at least $100. These accounts usually give you more money in interest than regular savings accounts. For example, a regular savings account might give you about 1% interest, but a high-yield savings account can give you 3% interest or more! However, you should be careful about taking money out of a high-yield account too often. If you take out money too often, the bank might change your account to a regular savings account.

The key is regularly saving and finding smart ways to help your money grow.

The 50/30/20 Budget Rule

Once you know where to save your money, you need to decide how much to save and spend. One helpful way to manage your income and expenses is using the **50/30/20 budget rule**. This rule suggests dividing your income into three categories: needs, wants, and savings. Specifically, you would spend 50% of your income on needs, 30% on wants, and 20% on savings. This simple approach helps you manage your money and ensures that every dollar you earn has a purpose.

For instance, if you earned $100 from mowing your neighbor's lawn for one month, you would divide your money using the 50/30/20 rule like this:

50% Needs = $50: These are expenses for living, like food, housing (shelter), or clothing.

30% Wants = $30: These are items that you desire but do not need, like toys, ice cream, skates, or going to the movies.

20% Savings = $20: This is the money you put away for future goals, like saving for a new video game, television, a trip to the bowling alley, or the mall.

Instead of spending the last $20, you would save it in your piggy bank or savings account to ensure it is kept safe for the future.

Using the 50/30/20 rule helps you divide your $100 so you do not overspend your money while saving for your dreams.

The Patience Game

Saving money takes patience, and it is important to remember that reaching your savings goals is a continuous process. Understanding that saving for your goals will not happen overnight can help you stay focused on long-term success. To remain patient, set short-term and long-term savings goals so you can break down your larger goals into small, manageable steps.

Creating small goals along the way can significantly boost your motivation. Small goals act as checkpoints that let you review your progress and help you stay on track. For example, if you have a long-term goal of saving for a new $400 smartwatch, consider breaking it down into smaller savings targets, such as $40 per month. When you reach $200 in savings, celebrate your achievement at the halfway point or when you have completed a particular month of savings. Remember, every little win gives you a reason to stay motivated and keep pushing forward.

What happens if you fall behind schedule? This might make you look at your spending habits and potentially save even more the next month. However, do not slow down on your savings goal if you save more than planned. Instead, consider saving even more. Saving extra can help you reach your goal quicker or can be used to start a new goal.

Remember to remind yourself of the reasons behind your savings goals. Whether it is for a special occasion, an emergency fund, or something you really want, keeping your goal in mind can serve as powerful motivation when you lose patience. When you feel tempted to spend your money, you can resist impulsive spending by reflecting on what you are saving for.

Patience, consistency, and the right savings strategies will ensure your saving journey is successful and fulfilling.

Chapter 4: Investing – Planting Seeds for the Future

Have you ever thought about how the money you save can work harder for you in the future? Once you have learned to budget and save, the next exciting step is investing! Investing means using your money to buy stocks and bonds, which can help you earn even more money as time goes on. Understanding the basics of investing can help you grow your money and reach your dreams, like buying a car, going to college, or taking a big trip. Samantha and Tiffany want to learn about investing because they think it will help them reach their goals in the future. Let's explore how you can make your money grow even more!

Types of Investments

You can put your money to work in different ways so that it grows over time. Some of the most common options are bonds, stocks, and ETFs (which stands for exchange-traded funds). Each of these choices has its own level of risk, which means some might be safer than others. For example, some **investments** are low risk, which means you are less likely to lose money, while others are high risk, meaning you could lose money but might earn more. It is important to think carefully about where you want to put your money so that it can help you in the future!

Bonds

While looking into bonds, Samantha learned that bonds are like loans people give to businesses or the government. When Samantha gives her money as a "loan," she earns interest, which is extra money, for a certain period, like one, five, or ten years. After that time, she gets back the money she originally lent, which is called the bond. Tiffany found this idea interesting, especially since bonds are considered a safer way to invest money than stocks. She realized that bonds could help her save and grow her money for the future!

Samantha explained to Tiffany that there are different kinds of bonds, but the most popular ones are government bonds. She learned that government bonds are backed by the government, which means they are safer, and she is less likely to lose her money. Tiffany thought putting her money in government bonds could be a good idea because it would help keep her savings safe while still earning a little interest.

I bonds and EE bonds are savings bonds that you can buy from the U.S. government. You can buy up to $10,000 worth of each type of bond every year. If you file your taxes, you can also buy up to $5,000 in paper bonds.

Even though you can buy a similar amount for both types of bonds, they are different in some important ways. This includes how much interest they earn, how they protect against **inflation** (when prices go up), and how they are taxed (how the government takes a portion of the money).

Key Differences Between I Bonds and EE Bonds

I Bonds

1. I bonds earn interest in two ways: a fixed rate that stays the same for the entire time you have the bond and an inflation rate that changes every six months based on how prices rise. That means if inflation increases, the amount of money you earn from the I bonds can also increase.

2. I bonds protect your money from losing value due to inflation. If inflation rises, the interest rate on your I bond increases, too, so your investment's value stays strong.

3. You need to keep I bonds for at least one year before you can cash them in. If you decide to cash them in before five years, you will lose the last three months' interest as a penalty.

4. The federal government taxes the interest you earn from I bonds, but there are no state or local taxes when you cash them in. You can also wait to pay your federal taxes until you cash in the bond or until it reaches its **maturity** date.

EE Bonds

1. EE bonds have a fixed interest rate and earn interest every month. If you keep them for 20 years, they will double in value. If they do not double in value by the end of 20 years, the

government will give you extra money to make sure they do.

2. You need to keep EE bonds for at least 12 months before you can cash them in. If you cash them in before five years, you will lose the last three months of interest you earned.

3. Similar to I bonds, you will not have to pay state and local taxes on the interest you earn on EE bonds. You also do not have to pay federal taxes on the interest until you cash them in or they reach their full limit (maturity).

I bonds are a good option if you are worried about prices going up (inflation), while EE bonds can be a steady way to save money for the long term. Choosing between them depends on what you want to do with your financial goals.

Exchange-traded funds (ETFs)

Are you willing to take some chances with your money if it could help you earn more later? What might that mean for your future?

Exchange-traded funds, or ETFs, are a type of investment that many people like because they balance risk and reward. ETFs combine different assets like stocks (shares of companies), bonds (loans to companies or governments), and commodities (gold or oil). Investing in ETFs helps you reduce the chance of losing a lot of money all at once while allowing you to profit as the market price of stocks, bonds, and commodities increases. ETFs usually maintain a steady balance, unlike regular stocks, which can go up and down a lot.

So, what is an ETF really, and should you consider it? You can think of ETFs as a salad bar where you can pick your favorite ingredients. Imagine going to a grocery store, looking at all the salads, and finding one that you like best. You might skip a salad that has olives and choose one with strawberries instead. That salad could have lettuce, tomatoes, strawberries, and blue cheese, among other things.

When you invest in ETFs, it is like buying a big salad made up of different ingredients. Instead of choosing just one kind of vegetable, you get a mix of things like stocks, bonds, and commodities. This way, you get a variety of investments all at once instead of having to pick each one separately.

Investing in ETFs can be easier than picking stocks on your own, just like buying a ready-made salad is easier than grocery shopping for each ingredient. Some ETFs let you invest in many different companies, while others focus on specific areas, like cars or technology. These can be exciting because they might earn you more money than other ETFs, but they can also be riskier.

Even though ETFs offer many choices, it is important to research them and find ones that match your goals. Spreading out your investments is a smart move. So, do not just buy the latest ETF because it seems popular. Take your time to make sure it is a good choice for your money because what seems good now might not always work out well in the end.

Stocks

Investing in the stock market can be a fun way to grow your money, but it is important to remember that buying stocks is risky. Stock prices can change based on how well a company is doing, how the economy is performing, and how people feel about it. Emotions like fear or excitement can have a big impact on stock prices. So, while you might make a lot of money, there is also a chance you could lose all your money. Before you start buying stocks, it is important to learn about the risks and to spend time researching each one carefully.

Samantha thought buying stocks was like owning a big pizza. When she bought a stock, she imagined she was getting a slice of that pizza, meaning she owned part of it. If the pizza had a bunch of toppings and were something that everyone really wanted, her slice would be worth more money, and she could make a profit. But if the pizza was something no one wanted or did not have many options (pepperoni, sausage, or stuffed crust), then she thought that many people would not be interested in buying it. This would cause the pizza company problems, and her slice could lose value, and she could lose her money.

Because of this, Samantha knew that looking up information about a company before buying a slice was very important. So before investing in stocks, she realized she had to check out the company's history, how well it was doing with money, and what it did (its business). She did not want to buy a stock just because everyone else was doing it. Plus, she wanted to understand how she could earn money from her investment when companies shared some of their profits through dividend payments.

Dividend Payments: Sharing the Profits

Some companies share their profits with their shareholders, who are the people who own part of the company through stocks, by paying them dividends.

Dividends are like bonus payments you get just for owning a piece of the company. Usually, companies that make a lot of money pay out dividends more often than those that do not. You can receive dividends in two ways: one, they can give you cash, which you can use to buy other stocks (pieces of other companies), or two, you can choose to reinvest them, which means they will put the money back into the stock you already own. This way, you own more of the same company.

However, many growing companies, especially new ones called startups, use their profits to grow instead. If a company does not pay dividends, it might use that money to create new products or hire more workers. Whether a company pays dividends or not depends on its future business goals and how much money it has. Understanding why a company pays dividends or reinvests its profits is crucial before you decide to invest your money in it.

Purchasing Fractional Shares: Investing with Any Budget

Have you ever wondered how to start investing in your favorite companies, even if you do not have enough money to buy a full share? Samantha and Tiffany, as beginner investors, had that same question. What if I told you that fractional shares could help you own a part of the companies you like, allowing you to invest just a small amount of money? Well, you are in luck because you can!

Fractional shares let you buy a piece of a single stock, even if you do not have enough money to purchase a whole one. Imagine a stock costs $100, but you only have $10. With fractional shares, you can buy 1/10th of that stock. Then, as you save more money, you can buy more fractional shares until you own a whole stock.

Additionally, if the stock pays dividends, you can also get a share of those payments based on how much of the stock you own, enabling you to continue building your **investment portfolio**.

Fractional shares make investing in expensive stocks easier for people with smaller budgets. They also help you diversify your portfolio by owning small pieces of many different companies. However, it is important to know that fractional shares carry the same risks as whole shares. If a company does not do well financially, your fractional shares will also lose value.

Understanding Risk

All investments come with some risk, meaning there is a chance you could lose some or all your money. The stock market is known for being unpredictable, with stock prices going up and down a lot in a short time. This can be tough for investors, especially if you are not ready to lose money or are focused on quick profits. In those cases, bonds might be a better choice because they offer greater stability and security. However, the safety of bonds often results in lower returns than stocks.

This is why **diversification** is so important. By spreading your investments across various assets – such as stocks, bonds, ETFs, and other securities – you can reduce the impact of poor performance in any single investment. For example, if one industry or sector struggles, other investments in your portfolio could do well, helping to reduce your losses.

It is also important to have a long-term goal when investing. While the stock market may make money over time, it can also result in losses in the short run. Market

fluctuations are normal, and maintaining a long-term view can help you stay calm during tough times rather than panicking and selling your investment quickly and at a loss. If you cash out your investments during a market drop, you might miss the chance to earn your money back when the market starts doing well again.

There is no single investment strategy that will work for everyone. Investing is not a "one size fits all" approach. It requires a unique, personalized approach based on your individual goals, how much risk you can handle (risk tolerance), and your financial situation.

Like saving, investing takes patience. Sticking with your investments through good and bad times increases your chances of growing your wealth.

Chapter 5: Stephanie's Saving Journey

Stephanie's family members' birthdays were coming up soon, and she wanted to give them gifts they would love. All their birthdays were within 90 days of each other: her mom's was in June, her dad's was in July, and her brother John's was in September. But her allowance was not enough to buy what she wanted, so she made a plan.

First, she decided to work harder around the house to earn more money. She told herself, "Five dollars a week," as she helped by feeding her pets Buster and Bella, cleaning Mittens' and Patches' litter boxes, and vacuuming the living room. It was not a lot of money, but every little bit helped. At the end of the first month, she had saved up $20.

Stephanie worked hard and took all her tasks seriously, especially when bathing Buster and Bella. She always took her time and gave them a spa-like treatment. She pampered the fur babies with top-notch grooming, keeping their fur coats healthy, shining, and always smelling fresh. Her neighbors, Mr. and Mrs. Brown often complimented her on how good of a job she did whenever she took Buster and Bella for a walk.

This gave Stephanie a great idea! One day, while walking Buster and Bella, Stephanie noticed Mr. and Mrs. Brown's puppies were covered in mud. She offered to give their puppies a bath at the low price of $15 and promised they would feel like they were at a spa. Mr. and Mrs. Brown accepted her offer! The agreement was for her to wash their two dogs twice a month for $15 each. This helped her earn an additional $60 per month for washing the Browns' dogs.

Calculating Stephanie's Dog Washing Income (1):

Beginning of the month
- $15/dog x 2 washes = $30

Middle of the month
- $15/dog x 2 washes = $30

- $30 + $30 = $60/month

Soon, other neighbors noticed how cute and clean the Browns' dogs always looked. One day, Mr. and Mrs. Johnson asked if Stephanie would provide the same service for their two dogs under the same agreement as Mr. and Mrs. Brown. She happily accepted their offer!

When Stephanie began her dog-washing business, she initially started with the Browns' two dogs. When she added the Johnsons' two dogs, her income doubled, adding another $60 to her savings.

Calculating Stephanie's Dog-Washing Income (2):

Beginning of the month
- $15/dog x 4 washes = $60

Middle of the month
- $15/dog x 4 washes = $60

- $60 + $60 = $120/month

So, every month, she earned $120 for washing dogs and $20 for her chores, totaling $140. In three months, she had saved $420! This was Stephanie's side hustle.

As her piggy bank became too small to hold all her money, she asked her parents to take her to the bank every two weeks when she earned money from washing dogs. She loved watching her savings grow and the interest she earned by keeping her money in her savings account.

With June approaching, she went to the mall to find the perfect gifts for her family. She found a beautiful $60 purse made of soft brown leather for her mom. Then, she spotted a shiny golf club for $87 for her dad to replace his old, rusty one. Finally, she thought of John and the Lego pirate ship he really wanted, which cost $25. She spotted it and added it to her cart. After these purchases, she had $273 left in her savings, allowing her to have some money left for her future goals. Perfect!

Using her version of the SMART savings plan – "Specific, Measurable, Achievable, Realistic, and Time-Bound" – she bought the gifts. As she wrapped them, Stephanie felt proud. It was more than just about buying presents; she thought about how she had earned the money to purchase them through hard work and a reminder of her love for her family.

Chapter 6: John's Saving Journey

John's eyes were glued to the screen, the vibrant graphics of the new "Galactic Guardians" video game bundle flashing before him. Two hundred dollars – that was the magic number. He knew his allowance would not be enough, but he was determined to make it happen. Using the SMART technique, he set his goal: Specific: Galactic Guardians bundle. Measurable: $200. Achievable: Save enough by December. Realistic: Save $70 a month. Time-bound: By December.

John's journey started in March. He earned a $5 allowance every week by mowing the lawn and helping his mom plant vegetables in their garden. But he wanted more money to reach his goal. To save more, he decided to offer lawn-care services to his neighbors. He went door-to-door and quickly got two regular clients, each paying him $30 two times a month to cut their grass. That added up to $120 a month from his yard work! This was John's side hustle.

Calculating John's Lawnmowing Income:

  Beginning of the month
- $30/cut x 2 yards = $60

  Middle of the month
- $30/cut x 2 yards = $60

- $60 + $60 = $120/month

John aimed to save $70 a month from his allowance and yard work. From March to October, his savings grew steadily. He kept track of his earnings and felt proud as the total increased. By the end of October, he had earned $1,120 from mowing grass and doing chores at home. He spent some of his money on summer fun with friends and clothes for the new school year.

November and December, the winter months, had arrived, and due to the cold weather, the grass had stopped growing. Because John was no longer cutting grass, his income fell to just $20 a month from his allowance. His heart felt a bit heavy, but he was not discouraged. He had saved carefully and still had a good amount of money left.

When December arrived, John walked into the video game store with the cash he had saved in his wallet. He bought the "Galactic Guardians" bundle, and a big grin spread across his face. He had done it! To his surprise, when he looked at his remaining money, he realized he had over $380 left. He had saved much more than his original goal! John felt proud of himself and was excited to keep saving, thinking he could buy a new game console next year. He daydreamed about all the fun he would have with the new console and the games he could play. John realized that by using the SMART technique and working hard, he achieved his goal and even went beyond it.

Chapter 7: Stephon's Budgeting Journey

Stephon is a smart 16-year-old who is making his way in the world. He landed a job as a cashier at the neighborhood grocery store, earning $15 an hour. Stephon worked 25 hours a week, which meant he was bringing in a good amount of cash. Now, the big question is: How does he manage it all?

Stephon wanted to be smart about managing his money and budgeting for the things that mattered to him: gas for his mom's truck (his need), some cool new video games and treats (his wants), and his prom (his savings). Prom was his biggest expense because he wanted to save for his tuxedo, a corsage, transportation, and tickets. That is where budgeting comes into play, and Stephon is about to learn how to make his earnings work for him.

Here is how Stephon calculated his money: He thought that if he worked 25 hours each week, he could make $375. If he worked four weeks a month and 25 hours a week, he could earn $1,500 each month.

Calculating Stephon's Income:

- $15/hour x 25 hours/week = $375/week
- $375/week x 4 weeks/month = $1500/month

Stephon wanted to split his money using the 50/30/20 rule. This rule helps him divide his earnings into needs, wants, and savings. Here is how he did it:

The Big Slice (50% - Needs):

- This slice is for the stuff Stephon *had* to pay for. For Stephon, the biggest need was gas for his mom's truck. He used it to get to and from work. That costs about $400 a month.

- **50%** of $1500 is $750. That is what Stephon *should* spend on needs. After paying $400 for gas, he had $350 left. Sometimes, he helped his mom with a few groceries at home. Other times, she told Stephon to keep the money, and he added it to his savings account.

The Fun Slice (30% - Wants):

- This slice is for the fun stuff – toys, video games, snacks, and maybe a new pair of sneakers he really wanted.

- **30%** of $1500 is $450. Stephon decided to spend $250 on some new video games and snacks for when he is hanging out with his friends. This left him with $200. He saved the leftover amount for a special occasion because he knew he did not always have to spend it all.

The Smart Slice (20% - Savings):

- This slice is for saving up for bigger things, like prom.

- **20%** of $1500 is $300. Stephon knew he wanted to look good for prom because it was the biggest high school dance. So, he saved $300 each month. He also decided to set aside some of his leftover money from his needs and wants to make his prom as memorable as possible and ensure he had enough for dinner at the end of the night. To do this, he added another $200 to his savings. This meant he had a total of $500 saved for prom!

Stephon remembered that saving his money was like planting a seed that required patience. He might not see a big tree right away, but over time, it would grow into something bigger to help him in the future!

Chapter 8: Julie's Investing Journey

Julie, a bright 13-year-old, dreamed of wearing a crisp white nurse's uniform and helping people heal. But she knew college was expensive and wanted to start saving early. That is where her mom came in – a savvy investor who believed in teaching financial literacy from a young age. Because of Julie's interest, her mom decided to open a managed portfolio account for Julie and transformed their home office into a monthly learning hub. Julie would excitedly bring her allowance savings to her mom every month, ready to learn more about stocks and fractional shares.

They had monthly meetings, which were a blend of learning and fun. Julie would often spot companies from TV commercials or recall her favorite toy brands. She would come to her mom with questions like, "Mom, remember that 'Super Soapy' laundry detergent commercial? Their stock symbol is 'SOAPS.' Can we buy some?" she would ask, her eyes sparkling with curiosity. Julie's mom patiently guided her through the research process, explaining how to analyze company performance, understand market trends, and consider long-term growth potential. They would explore the company's financial reports to see if they were making or losing money and discuss competing companies, like 'Sparkling Suds', to see how they compared to each other.

Julie started investing in companies she liked by buying fractional shares. She did not always have enough money to buy a whole stock, so her mom would say, "Even if a stock costs a lot, you can buy a little piece of it." This made investing easy and fun for Julie!

They also wanted to invest in companies that Julie liked, such as "Build-A-Block" toys and other products her family used. Her mom often talked about the importance of diversifying her investments. She explained that by spreading investments across different companies, people could lower the chance of losing a lot of money. Julie remembered her mom saying, "Don't put all your eggs in one basket!" This meant it was better to spread out your investments to help protect your money.

Each session ended with a review of Julie's portfolio's performance. They celebrated the gains and learned from the losses, always keeping Julie's college fund goal in mind. Her mom would remind her that "every share you buy is a step closer to your dream of becoming a nurse."

Julie thought the monthly meetings were about more than investing. They were about building her knowledge of investing, the value of patience and discipline, and the power of long-term planning. Through her mom's guidance, Julie grew her college fund and became confident and financially savvy. She also had enough money from her investments to pay for many of her college expenses.

Chapter 9: Your Financial Journey – A Bright Future Ahead

Reviewing the Basics

As you go through your financial journey, it is important to remember the basics of earning, saving, spending, and investing your money. Earning money can come from different sources, like an allowance, a business you started, or working for someone else. It can help you be more responsible and develop skills like budgeting and saving.

Once you get your first job, it is important to use the budgeting methods from Chapter 2. This will help make sure you have enough money for your needs, wants, and savings for future goals. It starts with setting SMART goals that help you understand why you are saving. Keeping these goals in mind can help you avoid overspending or making impulse purchases.

Once you understand why you want to save money, you can create a plan for growing your wealth over time. This plan might involve investing your hard-earned cash in savings bonds, stocks, or ETFs. You could also consider a safer alternative, like a savings account, to minimize the risk of losing money. By planning carefully and weighing the risks of investing against saving, you can gain a clearer vision of what you want your financial future to look like.

Ultimately, it is your choice to decide what you want for the future.

Building a Strong Financial Foundation

Building a strong financial foundation begins with developing good money habits at a young age and understanding the value of earning money. It is important to avoid buying something just because someone else has it or because a new toy has come out. Creating goals and sticking to them will help you become financially successful and resist temptation.

An essential step in building a strong financial foundation is saving regularly. Try to set aside a little money each week, whether in a piggy bank or a savings account. Remember, the more you save now, the more you will have to be able to purchase something special in the future!

Additionally, practice thoughtful spending: always consider whether you truly want an item and wait a day to see if you might change your mind, which can help prevent impulse buys.

Do not hesitate to ask an adult for guidance whenever you are uncertain about money matters. They can offer invaluable advice and share their personal experiences.

By embracing these habits, you are preparing for a financially secure future and learning the value of earning and managing money responsibly. Remember, every bit you save counts toward your bright and fulfilling future!

The Journey Continues

No matter where you are on your journey, continuing to learn and grow is important! Your life is exciting, and part of that adventure is discovering all there is to know about money. You will earn money, maybe even lose some sometimes, and you will also see your savings grow right before your eyes!

The amazing thing is that every challenge, like losing a bit of money, is a stepping stone towards becoming financially wise. Imagine you bought a new television, and soon after, a newer model comes out, or even worse, it stops working after a while. That may feel like a loss, but it can teach you big lessons about saving up for something even better next time!

The road may get bumpy, but with every step you take, you are closer to achieving your dreams. So, stay positive, focused, patient, and never give up. I also encourage you to continue to educate yourself, because knowledge is power. Keep pushing forward and remember that every small accomplishment is a huge victory. So, keep dreaming big because, one day, your hard work and determination will turn those dreams into reality – one amazing accomplishment at a time!

Definitions

50/30/20 Budget Rule: A method to divide and manage your money: 50% for needs (food, rent, housing), 30% for wants (games, movies), and 20% for saving or paying debt.

Compound Interest: Earnings on your savings that grow as you earn interest from month to month.

Counterfeit: A fake item made to look real, such as a fake dollar bill.

Diversification: Spreading investments across different types to reduce risk (stocks, bonds, ETFs).

Fluctuation: Changes that go up and down, like the price of gas or food.

Income: Money earned from work or other sources, such as an allowance or a side hustle.

Inflation: The increase in prices over time, making money buy less.

Interest: Extra money earned from saving money.

Investment: Putting money into something that may grow in value over time.

Investment Portfolio: A collection of all your investments (stocks, bonds, ETFs, mutual funds, etc.).

Maturity: The date when an investment pays back the money you invested.

Side Hustle: A way to earn extra money outside a main job or allowance, such as selling crafts, candy, or a car wash business.

Shareholders: People who own parts of a company after purchasing stock.

Acknowledgments

I extend my heartfelt gratitude to my husband, Dweise, whose patience, support, and diligent assistance were invaluable throughout the process of writing this book. His thoughtful suggestions for improvements and unwavering encouragement helped me thoughtfully consider my ideas. I am truly grateful for his partnership and belief in my vision. Thank you for being my rock!

About the Author

Annette Harris is a wife, mother, and avid volunteer in her community. She is a military veteran who spent eight years in the United States Army with two wartime deployments in Afghanistan and Iraq. She graduated from Florida State University with a Juris Master's degree and Webster University and Liberty University with Master's degrees.

She has worked as a human resource professional, an adjunct instructor in human resources, and is the owner and founder of Harris Financial Coaching.

She lives in Florida with her husband, Dweise.

Visit her website at www.authorannetteharris.com.

More Books from Annette Harris

The ABC's of Money for Little Spenders

From the Mommy, Can You Teach Me Series

Book 1: Mommy, Can You Teach Me About Money?

Book 2: Mommy, Can You Teach Me How to Save?

Book 3: Mommy, Can You Teach Me How to Budget?

Book 4: Mommy, Can You Teach Me How to Invest?

The Great Money Quest